A BIRD
IN THE
HOUSE

THE STORY OF WING HAVEN GARDEN

BY MARY NORTON KRATT

ILLUSTRATED BY LAURIE DOUGLAS

Wing Haven Foundation
Charlotte, North Carolina

Publication of this book was made possible by a generous gift to the Wing Haven Foundation.

Library of Congress Catalog Card Number 90-072015

ISBN 0-9628692-0-1

To make orders, inquiry, or donations write: The Wing Haven Foundation
248 Ridgewood Avenue
Charlotte, N.C. 28209

Book design by Laurie Douglas

In loving memory of
Ruth Simpkins Barrow
whose garden gave joy and strength
to all who partook of its beauty,
and whose life exemplified
love and generosity.
1892–1980

This book is the story of Wing Haven and of Elizabeth and Edwin Clarkson. During the decade of the 1980s, more than 40,000 people visited Wing Haven Garden in North Carolina. Magazines including *Audubon, Nature, House and Garden, Southern Accents,* and *Victoria* featured the extraordinary garden, which began in 1927.

A BIRD
IN THE
HOUSE

THE STORY OF WING HAVEN GARDEN

lizabeth Barnhill knew she would have a garden. As a child in Texas, she had watched her father, a banker, grow vegetables. She watched her mother and a Mexican gardener plant and prune roses and scatter larkspur and poppy seeds along barren Texas roadsides.

She knew she would probably raise small animals. She always had. As a young girl she raised a raccoon, a pig, and squirrels. Her brothers kept a coyote. Elizabeth told Eddie Clarkson on their first date in Boston, where he was working and she was attending the New England Conservatory of Music, how she and her mother had raised white-winged doves.

After five years of courtship in seven states and one foreign country, Eddie and Elizabeth became engaged. Eddie's father urged, "Don't let that pretty, little auburn-haired girl get away." Eddie proposed and drove his Essex auto to Uvalde, Texas in 1925 to give her an engagement ring. But before Elizabeth came to Charlotte, North Carolina in 1927 as Eddie Clarkson's bride, she mailed him her own design for the home she envisioned to complement their garden. It would be a simple two-story frame house with large windowed rooms which drew the outdoors in.

It would have a linear, wide-windowed kitchen where a servant could efficiently prepare meals and carry them to serve in the garden. Elizabeth planned a raised brick terrace off the double glass-doored living room where her piano could be moved outside for entertainments at candlelit garden parties. And when they had children, they would add rooms in flanking wings which would balance the vertical house.

During the fall before their marriage, Eddie received a tide of letters from Elizabeth in Texas which contained sketches and building instructions. With a Charlotte builder, Eddie carefully followed them. They included graceful details: a fan light with tracery over the sidelit front door and a newel post and stair exactly like hers in Texas. The house rose on a barren lot at the eastern edge of Myers Park, an elegant subdivision with gardens and wide curving streets begun in 1911. The early part of the neighborhood was designed by an eminent town planner, John Nolen of Boston. The land had once been the bare fields of a 1000 acre cotton farm. By 1927 the new, developing edges of the early, spacious curves of Myers Park reverted to a standard grid pattern of streets. The Clarksons' lot at 248 Ridgewood Avenue was a flat rectangle of broomsage with a straightforward house close to the street. There was hardly another house in sight.

When Elizabeth and Eddie arrived at the Charlotte train depot after their honeymoon in the spring of 1927, Elizabeth insisted on going immediately to the house and lot she had seen only in her imagination. Eddie slowed the car and stopped in front. Elizabeth gasped. The house stood stark and solitary in a field of hard, red mud with nothing green except a few waist-high pine seedlings . Eddie led her around back to the single tree, a spindly willow oak. Since Eddie did not have the door key to the house, they climbed in a window. He led her into the living room where his wedding present waited, a mahogany Steinway baby grand piano.

The next day Elizabeth started her garden.

CONTENTS

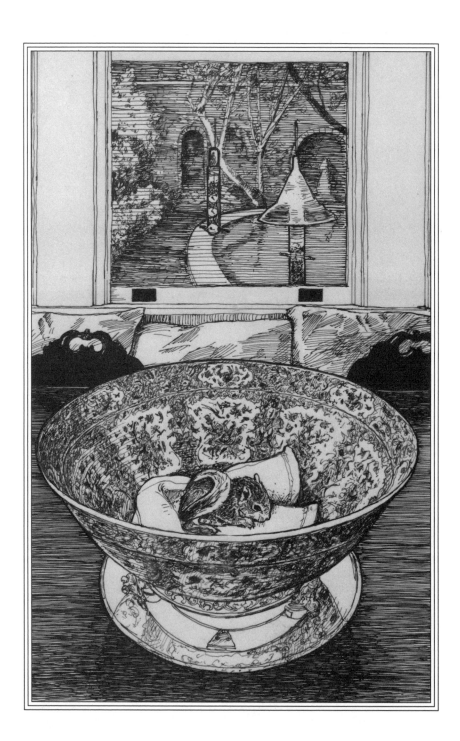

THE
GARDEN

year passed. The new six-inch hedge which sur-
rounded the main garden had just been closely
clipped when a school friend visited Elizabeth. The
friend laughed when Elizabeth referred to the mini-
miniature hedge and grassy rectangle as "my garden."

The friend could not see what Elizabeth envisioned,
the tall hedges, borders, the variety of trees, shrubs, and color,
nor could she yet smell the delightful scents or see the hidden,
welcoming places.

Occasionally, while Elizabeth worked in her "garden," men and women on horseback, out for a morning or evening
ride, stopped to ask what she was doing. They were Myers Park
neighbors exercising their horses along an old, dirt farm road that
led past the Clarksons' lot.

Elizabeth's young, ambitious plan called for a formal upper and lower garden with brick walls and long vistas.
Behind these would be a natural area with soft paths. Each plant
would be chosen for its contribution to the garden picture. The
proposed pools, walks, and six-foot walls with herb and flower
gardens would gradually follow. Eddie and Elizabeth began their

unique habit of gift exchange for birthdays and anniversaries, even Valentine's Day—always gifts for the garden: 1,000 bricks, mortar, bone meal, manure, or a brickmason's services for thirty feet of wall. In this way they built the outer brick wall one section at a time, then saved toward the next span. Between 1937 and 1942 the outer wall slowly crept around the entire property line of their large, visionary garden. They had persistently added seven small parcels of land. Since Eddie was in real estate, he kept a sharp ear and eye on the neighboring plots. Some came available in due course, but for others, they wheedled, bargained, and waited.

Some paths led straight to adjacent land they did not own, opened onto it like a hopeful question. Slowly it became theirs, and the more than three acre city garden, both the formal and the dense, rambling woodland, took form.

But misfortune struck. For a year Elizabeth lay ill with undulant fever, a bacteria-caused low grade fever which humans contract from an infected animal or from drinking unpasteurized milk. Elizabeth was confined to bed with headaches and recurrent pain, chills, and fever. The slightest exertion left her weak and exhausted. Since this occurred prior to the knowledge and use of antibiotics, the common treatment for the problem was bed rest and vitamins. Her illness persisted.

During her illness, Eddie kept a cot in the garden where Elizabeth lay most of each day when weather permitted. "Up until that time," said Elizabeth, "birds were just a lovely part of a garden's background and were taken more or less for granted." Lying there daily on the cot, she "felt suddenly I must know all about birds. A cardinal was singing immediately overhead and I realized I wanted, like Longfellow's "Hiawatha," to

> Learn of every bird its language,
> Learn their names and all their secrets,
> How they built their nests in Summer,
> Where they hid themselves in Winter.

12

Eddie Clarkson indulgently brought Elizabeth every book on birds that the Charlotte library possessed in both adult and children's departments. She began to collect books on birds, ordering them by mail. At first, for identification she used *Land Birds East Of The Rockies* by Chester Reed and a pair of eight-power Zeiss binoculars which she borrowed from a cousin.

But those long outdoor days of patient, minute observation were by far the best source of knowledge. Only watching and listening would reveal the various voices of one bird calling for different reasons, each species making numerous different sounds. The different color and look of young birds and their unique actions became familiar to her as did the adult birds' courtship rituals, chases, and territorial battles. She had the gift of time, of silence. She waited while the lives of the birds in the garden unfolded their secrets before her.

From then on, all additions to the garden were chosen from "the birds' point of view." The function of plantings extended beyond beauty to the purposeful attraction of birds. Elizabeth and Eddie once gave each other 5,000 mealworms as an anniversary present.

They planted mimosa, locust, mulberry, wild cherry, honeysuckle, elderberry, poke berries, Amur River privet, Chinese flowering crab apples (Alrosanguinea), Japanese weeping cherry and dogwoods to provide year-round berries and dense vegetation appealing to birds. They planted mahonia for spring berries favored by catbirds and robins; eleagnus would yield fall and winter berries. In one corner a field of grasses and wild flowers were allowed to go to seed for the birds.

In the upper garden they gradually added strawberries, raspberries, boysenberry, Mercereau blackberries, dewberry, loganberry and youngberry. Elizabeth wrote, "We eat a few and leave the rest to the birds." A wild plum thicket was carefully protected. They planted high bush cranberry, swamp-rose for hips, sumac, greenbrier, cedar, sarsparilla, chokeberry, black haw, barberry, sour gum, Virginia creeper and vitex, and numerous varieties of trees whose buds attract various species, such as goldfinch, siskins, and purple finches. For hummingbirds they chose larkspur, columbine, tuberoses, foxgloves, mimosa, clematis, and trumpetvine.

Miles Alexander, the Clarksons' knowledgeable gardener, taught Elizabeth all he knew about herbs and their medicinal properties. He had formerly collected herbs in the North Carolina mountains and had worked for an herb distributor in Statesville. He and Elizabeth built an herb garden for the 250 various medicinal and culinary herbs she gathered locally or ordered by mail. Miles also laid walks, helped to install three garden pools, ten birdbaths, three feeding stations, five suet baskets, and the numerous hummingbird feeders. Miles also transplanted 75 young dogwoods from native woods in other parts of Mecklenburg County, setting them out every ten feet within the garden's exterior wall. Every dogwood survived.

A feeding tray or hopper on Elizabeth's upstairs bedroom window offered sunflower seed on one end and mixed bird seed on the other. Her bedroom, like six of the house's seven rooms, had four curtainless windows. A large mirror on one solid wall gave her yet another outside angle of view. She could wake and watch the antics of both familiar and visiting birds, many of whom she and Eddie named for some individual peculiarity of the bird, such as Skinhead, Knock Knees, Patch-breasted Mama, Pale Male, Handsome, Straightforward, and Wasteful. Straightforward was a catbird who came back each spring and always looked guests straight in the eye. Wasteful, another catbird, habitually spilled several mealworms on the ground when she came to eat. Other birds ate what Wasteful carelessly dropped.

In Elizabeth's upstairs bedroom, shelves to the ceiling housed her growing collection of bird and garden books. In the upstairs rooms, Elizabeth preferred space to furniture, so she installed extensive built-in cabinets and shelves. She loved

14

elegant things, but kept possessions to a minimum, focusing on the garden. By design, the Clarksons' acquisitions were primarily friends (both animal and human) and books (antique, bird, and garden). One friend recalls being invited to one of Elizabeth and Eddie's dinner parties where guests were urged to take home one of the gift-wrapped packages by the door. They contained some of their wedding presents. "We don't need them. Take one home with you," Elizabeth said.

From the capacious feeders at windows upstairs and alongside the long dining room windows, birds enjoyed a continual feast. Elizabeth's bedroom window tray held a pyrex cup of peanut butter, a cup of water, a container of chopped American cheese, cracked walnuts and pecans, and half an apple. A hanging suet stick held peanut hearts and sunflower seed on peanut butter.

Such abundance yielded constant pleasures to the Clarksons and to the many neighboring children and visitors who continually stopped by. Hundreds of birds of many varieties were visible daily, feeding alongside squirrels and chipmunks. In the basement of their house, Eddie and Elizabeth initially raised what birds consider a rare delicacy, tiny, hard-shelled, crawly mealworms. The perishable mealworms (the larvae form of beetles) were kept in a dark, damp area of the basement in long, screened trays. Subsequently they ordered the mealworms and kept them in the refrigerator. The neighborhood postman recognized the boxes and brought them right in.

Elizabeth painted a tiny shallow can her favorite color, pink, and each day she carried it outside filled with mealworms. Birds would immediately swoop down and light on her head, shoulder, arm, and hand as she held it high. The birds knew exactly what they would find inside. Visitors delighted in this small, amazing pleasure.

But many visitors came for another reason. Elizabeth's knowledge of birds became well known. Neighbors and people all over town brought injured birds, or they carried into the Clarkson living room infant creatures blown out of their nests or abandoned. Elizabeth knew what to do.

She would take the bird to the dining room table and examine it just like on an operating table. In the deep Chinese rose medallion bowl on the dining room table, it was not unusual to find a fledgling reviving, a newborn squirrel, an injured baby rabbit, a robin nestling. The upstairs bathtub was frequently occupied by a creature on the mend, or perhaps wood duck babies whom Elizabeth was protecting from a marauding cat.

Her classic prescription to pep up an exhausted bird was a spider for lunch. A sure-fire tonic. Even while these creatures were being brought to her, Elizabeth urged at every opportunity, "Don't pick up baby birds! Harden your heart toward them. They need their mother. Find her. I have had baby birds brought to me nest and all." And for a bird who is stunned from flying against a window, she advised, "Watch and wait. Shoo away cats and dogs. Almost always the bird is stunned. Given time and no disturbance, he will usually recover and fly away."

Elizabeth liked cats, but not in her garden. They were the only visitors who were unwelcome. "You can't have birds and cats both," she said. "You have to choose. I chose birds. A cat will know when the baby wood ducks hatch. He will slip in and kill five or six at a time." One of the Clarksons' dogs, who was himself an injured stray, was trained for cat-alerts. Bradford ignored rabbits, squirrels, chipmunks, and even cotton rats, but when someone said, "Cats," he jumped to attention.

Depending on the bird's ailment, Elizabeth might send for berries from the garden at St. Peter's Episcopal Church, or prescribe some of her own herbs, or ask Eddie to stop by the Myers Park Pharmacy on his way home. For some birds, she put one teaspoon of antibiotic in a quart of water (occasionally with liquid vitamins), then placed some of the mixture in a fingerbowl for the small patient. It worked. Elizabeth became the quintessential Myers Park medicine woman. But she also called on physicians or veterinarians for advice or major assistance.

For other sick birds, constant attention was the key. One afternoon Elizabeth found a baby wood thrush nest with two live nestlings and a dead one on the ground. She put the nest back in place and watched from behind the shrubbery. The male bird came and fed the babies, but he was unwilling to sit on the nest and brood them for warmth overnight. The Clarksons put a hand warmer in the nest. At sunset the male went away and the birds were taken from the nest, placed in a warm basket and carried into the house. They were returned to the nest before sunrise so the parent would continue to feed them. With this alternating arrangement, the nestlings survived.

In 1932 Elizabeth began keeping records on what birds were seen in the garden. Over 150 species of birds were gradually recorded. Her book written in 1944, *Birds of Charlotte and Mecklenburg County, North Carolina,* (reprinted 1965, 1977, 1986) chronicled birds seen in the area and also gave basic information for learning about birds and specifically how to attract and protect them. It is hardly surprising that the founding meeting of the Mecklenburg Audubon Club was held at the Clarksons' in 1940.

All guests, both animal and human, were welcome at Wing Haven, and none more so than the lovely Eastern bluebirds. Bluebirds regularly enjoyed and raised their young in the pastoral edge-of-the-woods-and-fields setting of the Clarksons' hospitable garden.

BLUEBIRDS

I t started on a Sunday.

Watching from the window, Elizabeth and Eddie Clarkson saw trouble at the bluebird house. They knew that young nestlings had hatched in the box in the upper garden near the house. They watched as the adult male bluebird flew inside with worms for feeding the young, but flew out again with the worms still in his mouth. Then he tried again. Finally the male bluebird ate the worms himself. After waiting and hoping for the mother bird's return, the Clarksons realized she must have been hurt or detained. The victim of a BB gun perhaps. For some reason the male bluebird could not feed the young birds. Since the bluebird boxes were built with one side which opened, the Clarksons took the whole nest out. The nestlings were featherless, cold, and lifeless.

On that cold April day in 1936 when they brought the four tiny bluebirds indoors, the fledglings could not have been more than one day old.

Quickly the Clarksons placed a hot water bottle in the bottom of a wastebasket and set the nest of bluebirds down on it. Eddie dug earthworms and Elizabeth, with tweezers, fed

19

the water-dipped worm pieces, first into one open mouth, then into the next and the next. Eddie had to go to work in the morning, but Elizabeth kept up the feedings from daylight until dark every fifteen or twenty minutes. At first the tiny birds wouldn't lift their heads, they were so cold. Then each would lift its head slightly, open its mouth, then the head would fall back down. For two weeks Elizabeth kept feeding them continually. She said, "If I hadn't had a husband and a cook who were interested, I never could have raised them."

After she had been "caged" by her duties for two weeks, Elizabeth accepted a neighbor's offer to birdsit for her while Elizabeth went to a tea. She stayed the afternoon, but when Elizabeth returned, Mrs. Ginter, the kind neighbor, was on the verge of a nervous breakdown. She couldn't get any pieces of the worms into their mouths. "It is very hard to feed a small bird," said Elizabeth. "You have to be quick on the trigger."

Elizabeth knew she also had to keep the nest clean. She explained how a mother bird feeds them and then looks at them to see which one is going to leave its droppings. " I did the same thing. I could tell, because each tiny bird has a tendency to turn its end away from its brothers. Even if it is almost too weak to move, it turns toward the outside. So I got an after-dinner coffee spoon and held it under the one who would relieve himself. The fecal matter comes in a little sack, if the birds are healthy, and the mother flies away with the sack and usually drops it away from the nest so predators won't notice the droppings. When the young get older, they push themselves over to the edge of the nest and drop it over the nest's edge, but never in the nest, unless there is something wrong with the mother and she can't take care of it."

Throughout the eighteen days before the birds left the nest, the four tiny birds were insatiable. Some days Elizabeth was kept so busy, she did not change out of her nightgown.

The four bluebirds, whose eyes were closed initially, became lively and took on individual personalities. The Clarksons named them: Snuggler, Little Fellow, Lady, and Tommy. As the news of their presence spread, children, neighbors, and friends poured in to see the tiny guests in the crowded upstairs bathroom. And so it began. The Clarksons had no inkling what excitement lay ahead.

When the bluebirds began to flap their little wings, the Clarksons guessed they would soon leave the nest. "We went out and cut maple branches and tied them to the four poster bed. But they lit on everything else in the room but the branches."

Of the four tiny blue birds, Tommy was the precocious one. He left the nest first. Then Little Fellow, then Lady. But Snuggler didn't want to leave. He finally flew into the corner of an overstuffed chair and wouldn't even look out. He was scared to death.

Tommy took an early bath, on Eddie's bed, of course, and soon learned to fly up and downstairs. Snuggler preferred to burrow in a chair corner, perch cozily for hours on Elizabeth's shoulder, or hide in her long, auburn hair when she unpinned it. Certain favorite pastimes claimed all four birds, however, as they grew and moved freely in the house.

All four of them circled Eddie's gold pocket watch, which had been a wedding gift from Elizabeth. When Eddie took it off, it lay on his dresser. The birds watched intently as the second hand swept around. They pecked at it, tried to stop it, or to catch it. Then they took turns shaking the watch by its gold chain. Frequently they pecked at periods in the newspaper. If Eddie left an open book on the table, they persistently pecked each tiny dot.

Whenever Elizabeth played her piano, the bluebirds lit along her arms. On arpeggios they hung on for dear life, leaning back and forth as they would have on a swaying limb on the edge of an open field.

Soon the Clarksons fixed a three-foot screen box outside a window, hinging the screen so the growing bluebirds could fly outside. With her fingers, Elizabeth pushed wriggling earthworms into dirt-filled pans in the window box so the fledglings could learn how to feed themselves. Birds learn to hear worms burrowing and they would need that skill. For awhile, Eddie could not get to work at his real estate office before ten in the morning, because he had to dig for worms. Every evening he and Elizabeth trapped moths against the door screens near the porch light. When the couple attended garden parties, friends were never surprised to see bugs creep or fly from Eddie's pockets. Wherever he went, he collected live snacks for the bluebirds. He never came home without tidbits. Soon the bluebirds expected it and greeted him excitedly.

Only Tommy survived to spend a long life with the Clarksons. Snuggler and Little Fellow died of avian diptheria the first year. Lady lived several more. She had a withered hip, but was the most beautiful flier of the four. Like a swallow, she soared up and down the staircase. Lady lived with the Clarksons for several years, but Tommy stayed on as family for eight years, always sleeping in the house on his favorite book.

In the beginning he slept between *The Lincoln Library* and Roget's *Thesaurus*. His longest lasting choice was a large, orange volume, *The Book Of Wild Pets* in Elizabeth's bedroom bookshelves.

Tommy bathed in a soupbowl in the bathroom or in a fingerbowl in the dining room, never in regular birdbaths outside. He often startled dinner guests by taking a vigorous bath in the dining room fingerbowls. He flew to the fingerbowl's edge, lit, then impulsively jumped in, showering the linen tablecloth and everyone present around the dinner table. When Elizabeth's doctor saw Tommy land on Elizabeth's orange juice glass and take a drink, he warned, "You're going to have avian fever and T.B."

Tommy was a very healthy bird. He could eat 150 moths a day, or 40-50 grasshoppers. He even ate very large black grasshoppers which he caught outside and brought inside for his meal. Elizabeth described how Tommy ate. "He would always take a grasshopper (this was always on somebody's bed), and pull off the hind legs so it couldn't hop. He took it by the head and beat and beat and beat it until he got it soft enough to eat. I have seen him eat grasshoppers so big I thought he was going to die. He would sit on the foot of the bed and put his head straight up and hold it that way until the grasshopper could go all the way down. He wouldn't give up. We had an awful time in winter because there wasn't anything to feed him. He got so tired of earthworms." Eddie Clarkson never said that he got tired of digging for them.

Tommy lived inside completely for about one year. Subsequently, Tommy mated, but that remained outdoor business. He commuted outdoors to his bird family daily. They lived in the same birdhouse Tommy was born in. Whenever Elizabeth called him, he always flew to her. "Even dogs don't always do that," she said.

Elizabeth recalled, "When the bluebirds came to live with us, we had silk slipcovers in the living room. They were perfectly beautiful and I was so proud of them. There were no plastic covers at the time. But Eddie and I said, anybody could have new slipcovers and nobody could have an experience like this, so we decided to just enjoy it while we had it. So that's what we did."

A visitor, who was visibly shocked to see Tommy the bluebird soaring gaily around the living room, leaned against the doorjamb in fright and disbelief. "Oh," she exclaimed, "did you know there's a bird in your house?" Yes, Elizabeth certainly did.

The adventures of living with a precocious bluebird in the house made good reading in the daily newspapers. Tommy's antics became familiar knowledge to Charlotteans. They knew he liked to sing while the vacuum cleaner ran, and loved to fly away with pink kleenex or play tug-of-war with ribbons. They knew he gave photographers a fit, because he flitted from their cameras to their shoulders and heads and rarely stood still to pose. School classes came from far and near to meet him and have him sit on

their heads. When visitors sat on the living room couch, he came over and sat on them, looked them over, and talked to them in a very conversational bluebird language.

"While Tommy was mating, he would often see us in the yard," Elizabeth recalled, "and he'd fly down and light on us. The female just had a fit because she thought we were going to harm him. It was miserable for her."

Perhaps Tommy's most unusual act derived from his instinct to feed young. He often brought an earthworm or grub worm to Elizabeth. "I knew what he wanted," she said, "because I'd heard bluebirds make that sound when they have something in their mouth. I knew what he wanted so I would hold two fingers together and he would put whatever he had in my hand. Then he'd take it back. I'd make that little noise and he would walk all around and make that noise again and put it back in my hand. This happened in the spring, every spring. On another occasion," Elizabeth recalled, "one day when I was dozing, I heard that little sound, opened my eyes, and he had this big black spider in his mouth and was getting ready to feed me!"

A visiting journalist for *Nature* magazine wrote, "Tommy was the first bird I have known to try to feed a person. Elizabeth would hear him give his little call, which meant he had food for her. It was the same note a parent bird gives when bringing food for nestlings. Mrs. Clarkson would make a noise with her fingertips, similar to that made by little birds with their bills. Tommy would fly to her hand and press the food into the space made by holding a finger against a thumb. Then satisfied, he would fly away and sing."

Whenever Tommy was not as perky as usual, Elizabeth, Rosetta, and Eddie searched for spiders to feed him. They were like a tonic for him. He immediately felt better.

Several times he almost died because of his mischievousness. He stole a needle once, but it was retrieved. He had a penchant for rubber bands which almost did him in. Once when

Elizabeth had severe hayfever, her doctor had instructed her to place a glass slide on her windowsill in order to catch a sample of pollen. She removed a rubber band from the box containing the slide. Tommy stole the rubber band and swallowed it. All remedies failed (including mineral oil, whisky, and probing gently with a small crochet hook). Finally a Charlotte surgeon agreed to operate if Elizabeth would supply a cross section diagram of a bird's physical structure. An hour before the doctor was due, Elizabeth was sitting by Tommy, when he suddenly slumped over with his mouth open. She grabbed the tip of the rubber band from his mouth before it could go back down, then called the doctor to thank him for his willingness.

His love of rubber bands almost killed him several times. William R. Taylor lived on a nearby street and because he had a degree in poultry science, occasionally got calls from the Clarksons. He had operated a large poultry business in Charlotte for several years and also raised and exhibited show birds.

One day Eddie called Bill Taylor, "Can you come and see what's wrong?" Tommy hadn't eaten in five days.

"We sat down and observed the bird. He was gasping. I held him and examined his throat. With my forceps I found a piece of rubber band in his throat. He got well immediately."

Elizabeth remembered one particular day in December. "Tommy was eight years old, but he really wasn't old. It was my father's birthday about 7:30 in the morning. Lying in bed, I heard a little scratching. Tommy heard it too. It frightened him and he flew out of the bookcase into the window shade. I thought he barely hit it, but he fell straight down to the floor. I picked him up and he died in my hand."

For the remainder of her life, Elizabeth told garden visitors the stories of the four bluebirds who stayed. But especially she told about Tommy, who splashed in dinner guests' fingerbowls and always came whenever she called, "Tommy, where are you, boy? Come, Tommy."

OTHER GARDEN STORIES

Throughout the life of the garden, Elizabeth Clarkson, the storyteller, told strange and amusing tales of the many birds and small animals who stayed or visited Wing Haven over a period of sixty years. As children around the Pied Piper of Hamlin or chicks around a mother hen, adults and children alike listened in wonder. They followed wherever Elizabeth walked.

WRENS

Elizabeth described the Carolina wrens in this fashion, "The song of a Carolina wren starts small and melodious, swells to a crescendo, transforming the whole house and garden. You have no idea how loud a wren is until you hear it in a small room. The walls expand to this most remarkable sound."

One beautiful April day, the Clarksons hurried around the house preparing for special houseguests who were to arrive on Holy Saturday, the day before Easter. Dr. and Mrs. Arthur Allen of New York were regular guests at Wing Haven and were to stop by as usual on their way to Florida. Dr. Allen was a noted ornithologist at Cornell University. He and his wife particularly enjoyed the balconied upstairs guestroom which overlooked the garden.

But several days before they arrived, Elizabeth noticed two Carolina wrens coming in and out of the tiny hole on the inside stairway at the landing. The pert brown wrens with the distinctive white stripe over their eyes flitted here and there into every cranny in the guest room, investigating even the closet, searching for a nesting place. Elizabeth put a deep, square basket on its side in the bookcase and waited to see what would happen. The female wren began building her nest in the basket while the male perched inside the room and sang. The Clarksons watched both wrens import moss, small twigs, and straw.

When the Allens arrived, the Clarksons had to tell them that there was an unexpected dilemma. Elizabeth said, "I am sorry I can't offer your favorite room, but we have previous guests."

Not long afterward, the mother wren laid five eggs in the bookcase basket and hatched them. Elizabeth feared the baby wrens would not be able to find their way out of the house, so she placed a luggage rack beside an open window. The mother wren led her babies perched on the rack to a lombardy poplar and later, enticed them back inside the hole for the night.

It was not at all unusual for the Carolina wren to light on the candles in the dining room, to appear in the kitchen for a mealworm snack, or to conduct an aerial search for spiders in every tall corner of the house.

Elizabeth declared that the tiny, tidy wrens "never dropped anything in the house as long as they lived with us except for one leaf when a mother wren built her nest in the bookcase."

Another visitor, Carl W. Buchheister, a former president of the National Audubon Society, described his stay at the Clarksons'. "One of the most delightful and charming experiences of my Audubon career was to be awakened in the guest room by a Carolina Wren, one of Wing Haven's greatest songsters! Before retiring the night before, I discovered to my surprise a dish of meal worms outside the guest room door on the newel post at the top of the stairs, a breakfast provided for the Carolina wrens. The birds made their entry into the house through a special aperture in the bottom of the window frame. In no other bird sanctuary in our country do birds have the run of the owners' home and the privilege of having a nest behind Latin texts on the guest room bookshelf!"

Elizabeth had called a carpenter to fashion a special, round upstairs entrance beneath the stairway-landing window for their bird guests. It was a very small opening, primarily for wrens or bluebirds. But later, all the garden birds discovered the hole: mockingbirds, towhees, cardinals, catbirds, titmice, and others. Occasionally they fought and chased each other inside the house just like unruly children. Elizabeth feared they would hurt or kill themselves against her many mirrors or break the prize Royal Worcester birds which English artist Dorothy Doughty modelled of myrtle warblers in the Clarksons' garden.

The carpenter was summoned again, and he built a slender, lucite box, that opened to the outside only. The birds could feed and be viewed without free run of the house as before. Sadly, there would be no more wrens, nesting and singing in the bedroom.

Several years in springtime, the Clarksons' back door leading from the kitchen to the main garden was locked, an unprecedented action for the hospitable household. This door also was the main utility entrance for supplying the feeders as well as the door to carry meals into the garden. But Elizabeth's note on the door was firm, "Please do not open this door." In an old-fashioned basket hanging just outside the door, a Carolina wren had chosen to build her nest. She came and went constantly, feeding her young. Her task took priority over all other needs of house and garden. She must not be disturbed.

WOOD DUCKS

"Eddie and I used to go to New York every fall," said Elizabeth, "to attend national ornithological meetings, but we always called home to leave our phone number. Anytime there was an emergency, such as the wood ducks' hatching, we came right home." But it soon got to the point that Eddie stopped making trip reservations. The vulnerable wood ducks were a particular concern, those hatched in the garden as well as the fledglings others brought to them from farm ponds where foxes prowled or lakes where a predator killed the mother.

One friend gave the Clarksons a pair of wood ducks named Bride and Beau. They grew tame and nested in the wooded recesses of the garden. In the fall, the young migrated, but survivors returned annually to feed and raise their young in the special nesting boxes high in Wing Haven's trees. The boxes were made of air conditioning pipe painted to blend into the rustic surroundings. Elizabeth filled them partially with sawdust and lined them with wire fabric to help the young ducks climb out. (Normally wood ducks nest high in hollow trees.)

As Elizabeth watched quietly from a bench in the garden, a family of wood duck nestlings hatched in the box. When they were ready, one brave nestling poked his head out, procrastinated, then dropped the long distance to the ground and shakily staggered away. Like paratroopers jumping from a plane, the others plunged one by one from the nest.

Another year, a friend brought wood duck eggs and nestlings to the Clarksons when turtles and large-mouth bass pursued them on his farm pond. At Wing Haven the ducks had a far better chance for survival. Because the Federal Migratory Bird Treaty Act prohibits possessing native birds or their eggs, feathers, or nests, Elizabeth secured a permit allowing her to assist birds in regaining their healthy wild existence.

Another wood duck mother took her fifteen-day-old young out of the garden. While the mother went seeking food, a cat stalked the young ducks, so two small, alert girls caught all of them in a pasteboard box and returned them to Elizabeth. She was quite distressed because young wood ducks attached to a mother were creatures Elizabeth never put her hands on. "I'd love to, but I don't dare," she said. She put an old feather duster on top of the little ducks, but that did not please them at all. When the mother flew in about dusk and called, Elizabeth put the ducks where the mother could hear them. Holding the box on the ground, Elizabeth tilted it gradually as the mother came nearer.

"They just flowed right under her. It was wonderful."

Another of Elizabeth's mother ducks, a returning resident, led her young out of the garden. (Mother wood ducks often move their young for protection.) A professor from nearby Queens College called to say a female wood duck had been killed on a busy street and had her eleven babies with her. Elizabeth and a neighbor hurried and found the mother lying with one dead baby at the curb. The ten others had obviously scattered and were nowhere in sight.

Knocking on the doors of nearby houses, Elizabeth asked if she could go into the backyards and search. Meanwhile, other helpers were already in backyards searching. They herded most of them into one woman's garage. The woman emerged from her house demanding querulously, "What do you think you're doing in my garage?"

"We're catching wood ducks." Dubious until she saw them, the woman pitched in to help. They caught all but one.

Elizabeth became the mother of the orphaned wood ducks, and at each stage of their growth, she adapted to accommodate them. When they were old enough to swim, she and Eddie put low chicken wire around a tiny terrace pool beside the house. An adjacent cage served as protection from the weather. There the ducks ate and slept, came out to swim and sun. But every night when the small ducks were brought inside for protection, Eddie

siphoned out the pool, scrubbed the inside, and poured fresh water for the next day. This went on for weeks. "I've raised lots of ducks," said Elizabeth, "and I love to do it, but it's awfully hard work. I would not advise anyone to raise birds." But for the Clarksons who had both the skill and patience, the rewards were obvious.

Irving was definitely worth the trouble. When city treecutters found two baby wood ducks in the trunk of a fallen tree, they took them to the Charlotte Nature Museum. The director felt they probably were wood ducks from Wing Haven and took them to Elizabeth right away. The injured one died that day, but the other survived and was named Irving after Irving Johnson, a good friend of Elizabeth. The rationale was that whatever the duck's sex the name would be appropriate. Irving, as it turned out, was female.

To teach the small wood duck to eat, Elizabeth pecked at a live mealworm with her finger. She talked to Irving, kept her in a soft, warm place with food and water outside. Soon Irving was old enough to swim in the small, protected pool. She dived and swam around beneath the surface "like she was never coming up, then popped up like a cork and flapped her miniature wings." With a showman's sense of timing, she delighted visiting garden clubs and children.

Elizabeth raised Irving like a pet, teaching her what she would need to know. She protected Irving from cats, but otherwise let her do as she pleased. One day an adult female wood duck flew in, returning from migration. Irving was afraid and ran to her cage, then gradually emerged. The two ducks swam together in the pool.

On cool evenings, Irving climbed into a particular lounge chair beside the Clarksons in their regular evening time in the garden. Irving listened as they read to each other from the newspaper, the classics, or the Episcopal prayer book.

Since cats could force a paw through the cage, Elizabeth continued bringing Irving in at night. When Irving began to fly, Elizabeth removed the cage and let her do as she chose day and night. What she chose was to come in each night as before. She came to the garden door, entered through the living room, paused to admire herself in the mirrored base of a table, then climbed the stairs, one step at a time, to her room to spend the night. She wanted to sleep on the bed. Irving's cage, when she was small, had sat on the bed with plastic beneath the cage and the bedspread. So Elizabeth put newspapers in the places on the bed where Irving wanted to sleep. Irving was a very particular guest.

Early every morning the Clarksons opened the sliding doors to a small deck from Irving's room (the guest room), so she could leave at her leisure. Eventually she went out to the edge of the second floor deck overlooking the main garden. She preened every feather carefully, then flew down onto the pool.

"People are always shocked when I say I had a duck in the house," Elizabeth later recalled. "But if Irving wanted to come in to sleep, I did not have to put food or water in with her if we were going to let her out early the next morning. Ducks usually come in at dusk. They won't mess things up."

Elizabeth never tried to keep Irving in the house once Irving learned to fly. Tame with Elizabeth and Eddie, Irving gradually became frightened of other people and flew off periodically. Elizabeth worried as hunting season and migrating time approached. She could tell that Irving was afraid of owls. When the barred owl was in the garden, Irving sensed it was there although she could not see it. She came to the door and wanted to be let in and to eat. Elizabeth gave her all she wanted, then Irving went out again.

As fall approached, Irving disappeared more frequently, then flew away for winter migration. The following spring Elizabeth watched, hoping each day would bring her safe return.

Late one evening, two female wood ducks flew onto the pool. Elizabeth went outside and called in the same manner she used to summon Irving. One female swam closer, halfway across the pool, and called an answer, Irving's answer. Elizabeth was satisfied.

Not long afterward, Elizabeth lay reading in bed in her airy, upstairs bedroom where the entire garden and its large pink crepe myrtle tree are visible. Elizabeth looked up from her book. In the mirror she saw a wood duck sitting on the deck rail looking in. "I knew it was Irving because no other wood duck would do that. I went down to the pool outside where she was swimming with a male. The duck answered with the female wood duck's loud, wild yell." (The female wood duck is the loud mouth of the pair. The male gives a low ssss-ss-ss.)

Irving swam to within fifteen feet of Elizabeth. The male flew away. Not long afterward, Irving brought a row of wood duck comrades to line the upper deck railing. They looked steadily at Elizabeth in her bedroom, observing her from without, as Elizabeth had so often watched Irving from within.

On other evenings as darkness drew close, a pair of wood ducks came silently onto the tiny pool against the house where Elizabeth and Eddie had raised so many young ducks, where so many learned to paddle and preen. Something brought them back, some slender thread of memory.

ROBINS

One summer day two little boys from nearby Croydon Road labored up the walkway. Between them they carried a great washtub with one tiny baby robin rolling in the bottom. They wanted Elizabeth to take care of it. She listened as they explained at length their decision not to carry the foundling in their hands. They felt it would be very bad for her. How could anyone refuse? Elizabeth already had a house full of birds, rabbits, and a dog. "I didn't need another bird to raise," she recalled.

After Elizabeth nursed the robin for about two weeks, she introduced the robin to a neighbor who had three young children, all boys. The friend asked, "Is it a girl? You know,

I've never had a girl named after me." So they called the robin Cousin Jane.

Elizabeth described Cousin Jane as a first rate character. Her favorite perch was on a jar of pink hand lotion or on a mirror. Jane delighted everyone. She lived in the house at first, then came back and forth for food. Jane's picture appeared in *Audubon Magazine*. But after she nested and became a mother, she no longer came into the house.

Fan, a subsequent resident female robin, claimed her name by fanning her tail and dancing. She was a most ladylike bird who loved to experiment with lipstick. Elizabeth, whose favorite color was pink, had a different color of lipstick for each dress. Inside her drawer a special holder held the lipsticks without their tops. If the drawer were left open even momentarily, Fan lit on the drawer edge and dipped into a lipstick, then wiped it off on whatever was handy, the bedpost, the sink, the bathroom curtain—so much easier than cleaning it on a crumb. Her favorite color was Pink Lightning.

One cold December day, a neighborhood postman on his morning route found a sneezing, gasping robin. As was his custom, he took the ailing bird to Elizabeth. When she first touched the robin, she was alarmed. Instead of the usual plump breast, she felt a sharp bone beneath his chest feathers.

She treated the emaciated robin for pneumonia with antibiotics and liquid vitamins. But after he gradually recovered in the warmth and care of the Clarksons' home, Elizabeth was afraid to release him in the unusually cold weather. She feared he would sicken again because of the sudden contrast in temperature. So Elizabeth appealed to anyone going to Florida to give the robin a ride. Local newspapers carried her request and the Clarksons' phone rang constantly. One caller was a ramp supervisor for a major airline who had cleared the bird's passage with his superiors. Two employees hand-carried the bird in its box and released it in a residential area of Miami.

Newspapers up and down the Atlantic seaboard described the robin's safe arrival and displayed his photo: "Robin flies the wings of man first class." His photo was published and letters poured into Wing Haven from persons who read of the event.

TOWHEES

"Handsome, a male towhee, was one of the most beautiful birds I ever saw," declared Elizabeth. His smart orange and black feathers with a bit of white always shone like satin. He was so tame, he jumped on her hand, turned his back to her, and looked all around to be sure nobody would attack him from the front. He seemed to realize that Elizabeth presented no threat.

Elizabeth described Handsome as an example of how tameness in birds differs, some eating from a person's hand, others distrusting. Handsome claimed an extra privilege of friendship by coming in through the special hole in the house which the wrens used. Once when he found no food upstairs near the opening, he flew downstairs and approached Elizabeth. She brought mealworms from the kitchen, calling "Come on, Handsome." He hopped up one stairstep each time she took a step until he ate from her hand at the top of the inside stairs. When he ate his fill, out he flew again.

Handsome died on Elizabeth's bed as she sat beside him. One stroke followed another. First his right side became paralyzed, so he hopped on his other leg. He held his wing even though he could not use it at all. He began to recover, but had several more strokes. Realizing he was not going to live, Elizabeth had brought him inside the house just before he died.

Broken Wing, another male towhee, had a badly broken wing. Elizabeth saw him for the first time as he came through a hole in the garden wall, his wing almost to the ground. He had babies on the other side, so she started to feed him to help him out. He approached stealthily under the bushes to avoid notice, climbed up through the dense privet hedge until he could rise high enough to hop onto the cedar limb. Then he hopped from one limb to the next until he gained sufficient height to hop to Elizabeth's bedroom window. To help him, she went outside and met him with food.

With his major handicap, feeding small offspring proved a great hardship for Broken Wing. The wing did heal, but from then on he flew at an angle. Several birds at Wing Haven lived out their lives with injured wings. Elizabeth observed that if a bird's wing is slightly damaged or hurt, it may heal itself if the bird is protected and fed while recovering.

CARDINALS

The Frog Hollow Cardinal was a longtime friend whom the Clarksons knew in their garden for thirteen years. When they met, he had come in search of food for his young. Because he had a slightly broken wing, Elizabeth helped by throwing worms near him. As his wing healed on his own, he gradually came to eat from her hand. Their friendship continued through generations of offspring.

His territory was Frog Hollow, a shady, hidden spring deep in the garden where royal fern, jack-in-the-pulpit and solomon's seal grew. He considered all that territory his, but it overlapped that of another cardinal, the Pale Male. The two cardinals fought for years. When they settled and built their nests, there was a general peace, but if one crossed the other's territory, a fight inevitably followed.

The Pale Male fathered generations of young cardinals who weren't always as pale as he. One daughter, called Palomino by the Clarksons, was the color of bleached bone. One day while a group of women held a club meeting in the garden, Palomino flew down and lit nearby. No one could talk of anything except the extraordinary bird. Her presence totally ended the meeting.

Because of her unusual color, Palomino had a difficult time getting a mate. She had a succession of "husbands" for several years. Finally she settled in with Bald Head, who couldn't get anybody either. Bald Head courted each female that passed but had been singularly unsuccessful. When he and Palomino finally mated, they became a match for life. The Clarksons observed that most birds do not mate for life, but this pair did.

The last time Elizabeth saw Bald Head, he was very old. The other birds had pushed him out of the garden completely, so his territory lay far beyond the wall. Palomino followed him because he was her mate, but they sneaked often to the feeders for food.

Elizabeth recalled the last time she saw the Frog Hollow Cardinal. He had come through a hard winter and hopped feebly along the brick garden path to eat from her hand. She said, "My goodness, old man, I am afraid I will never see you again." She never did.

The cardinals lived at Wing Haven year round and had a large progeny. One was an orange cardinal, not quite the color of a Baltimore oriole. Visitors, including noted bird photographer Fred Truslow, came back from walking the paths, and asked Elizabeth, "Did you know you have an orange cardinal?"

Familiar pairs of cardinals resided consistently at Wing Haven and ate from Elizabeth and Eddie's hands almost every time the couple went outside. Eddie observed, "In winter most male and female groups don't stay together. In the fall the male cardinal feeds the female so tenderly, but in winter he'll knock her off the feeder."

HOMER THE GRACKLE

As Elizabeth and Eddie looked from the windows one cold, threatening April day, they had a premonition something extraordinary was about to happen.

Near the pool in the main garden, a purple grackle

pecked rapidly at something in the grass. Knowing grackle activities are not always above reproach, they hurried toward him. A large, old bullfrog clung tenaciously to the grackle, whom they knew was about one week out of the nest. By the time the Clarksons reached the pool, the frog had dragged the young bird into the water. Maneuvering a long-handled crabnet, they landed both frog and grackle and separated them. They laid the young grackle on the grass. He shivered as though breathing his last. Wrapping him in a towel, they put him very briefly in a warm oven with the door open.

He revived slowly and ate a few bits of scrambled egg. All day he ate small bites of egg and worms from tweezers, but Elizabeth had to pry open his mouth to feed him. With a medicine dropper, she gave him water. By night it was clear that he would be none the worse for his unusual ordeal. This was the beginning of Homer.

Homer became a well-known and publicized Wing Haven character. He was adopted by a sixth grade class whose teacher, Laura Owens, had special interest and expertise with birds and animals. As the willing focus of a bird study, Homer occupied a special screen-wire house in Laura Owens' classroom. He enjoyed celebrity write-ups in the newspapers and in *Audubon Magazine* (July, August, 1945). He learned tricks, took part in a school play, and graduated as the class valedictorian. Elizabeth felt that the most remarkable thing about Homer was that he spent each weekend with a different child and survived.

FROG

Meanwhile, a very old, large frog lived for many years in the main garden pool under the graceful pink crepe myrtle. Often he caught birds (like Homer) and dragged them back and forth under the water until they stopped fluttering. He could not eat them unless they were very small, but he thought he could.

Once he crept up stealthily behind a large dove. The

dove raised her red feet, flapped her strong wings loudly, and with a long, tremulous whistle escaped from danger.

After this sinister frog caught five birds in this manner, Elizabeth drained the pool. She planned to deport him to the creek the next day. Chagrined and concerned, she debated overnight, and reluctantly decided against deporting him. For some odd reason, the frog never repeated his violence.

DAPHNE THE RABBIT

Elizabeth and a friend, whose garden she was designing, went shopping for shrubs at a nursery. They noticed a small, white rabbit running free beneath the plants. The nurseryman explained that the rabbit had belonged to his daughter. She got tired of it, so he let it loose. Seeing the two women's delight in the rabbit and knowing its potentially destructive appetite, he offered it to the ladies as a bonus. They brought the young rabbit home.

That evening a neighbor asked Elizabeth, "Well, what did you buy?"

"Two pyracantha and two daphne," answered Elizabeth. Eddie corrected, "Three daphne."

The first few weeks Elizabeth kept Daphne in the corner of the dining room on thick newspapers surrounded by a makeshift fence. When let loose, Daphne and the dog Bradford chased each other through the house and upstairs. (Bradford had also been a foundling. The Clarksons rescued him, an exhausted, mange-ravaged derelict puppy lying in the gutter in front of the Bradford Gynecological Clinic.)

Elizabeth enjoyed keeping roses in the old Chinese bowl on the piecrust table, but Daphne liked to get up on the chair to eat the roses. Elizabeth called, "Bradford, stop Daphne." Consistently Bradford made Daphne get down. As a reward Bradford received a toy from his drawer in the living room chest.

Later, Daphne established her own domain in the

kitchen closet where her papers and food stayed. Bradford knew he was unwelcome there. Elizabeth put food dishes on newspapers since rabbits predictably go to the bathroom right after eating. Daphne did not litter beyond the paper. She ate oats, rabbit pellets, sunflower seeds, greens, wild grains, and grapes from the bottom shelf of the refrigerator. Poison ivy was one of her favorite foods. She thrived on it. She also liked the taste of the ink on *Newsweek*. It was the only magazine she ate. In the kitchen if she wanted something, Daphne beat her food pans against each other until she got attention.

Daphne's behavior supported Elizabeth's belief that rabbits are smarter than humans believe. Daphne could discriminate in many ways. There were several people she disliked enough to consistently wet on them. When children pestered Daphne, she flattened herself and slid under any object to hide, until she later got too large to do so.

One summer, when the Clarksons were overrun with cockroaches and had to move out during fumigation, a neighbor offered to keep Bradford overnight while they went to a motel. "I'll keep the dog," she offered, "but not the rabbit." This neighbor was one of the people Daphne always wet on. The large, sixteen-pound rabbit was difficult to smuggle into a motel room. (There was a $50 fine for keeping animals in the room.) Daphne didn't like such confinement, so she noisily banged her pans. Her conspicuous presence made it even more difficult for the Clarksons to smuggle her out in daylight, but as usual, they managed.

Daphne and Bradford were constant companions, buddies even, and the Clarksons' house was their own. They had access to all visitors, so when the Clarksons' house and garden were open for the Mint Museum of Art's annual garden tour that spring, the rabbit and dog were part of the tour. Elizabeth and Eddie worried over the prospect of managing Daphne, Bradford, and the constant visitors. The rooms and flowering yard glowed in the flickering candlelight and a profusion of pink sultanas.

46

People entering the front door occasionally noticed and were startled by Bradford and Daphne lying under the dining room table. Several men crawled under the table to pet Daphne.

Daphne lived seven years with the Clarksons. When Bradford died one February, Daphne searched the house for him. She died one month later.

DOGS

Elizabeth named several of her evolving family of dogs after the girls in her wedding. "They didn't appreciate it either." But Pudgy, a fluffy, mixed fox terrier wasn't named for anyone. He looked like a pudgy collie puppy. One couple came to look the foundling over for possible adoption, but turned him down. The Clarksons were insulted, but later were grateful because Pudgy lived with them eighteen years. He and his brother, Kino, were buddies. When Elizabeth began playing the piano each day, they ran to the living room, put their paws on the bench, one dog on each side of her. She commanded, "Sing, boys, sing!" They howled together. When they finished singing, they ran to the refrigerator for the reward that always followed their performance.

Pudgy and Kino weren't much help when the Clarksons brewed homemade beer and lined 150 bottles along kitchen surfaces to await capping. Pudgy and Kino got in a fight and knocked over all the bottles. Beer flooded the floor. Since the only way to stop the fight was by throwing water on the struggling dogs, this left the sopping kitchen inches deep in diluted brew.

Among the Clarksons' succession of housedogs was an Irish wolfhound named Sylvia. The last dog they owned was a white toy poodle. They named him Folly because, as Elizabeth explained, "in old age it's folly to have a dog like this."

OPOSSUMS

One summer evening someone brought a most unusual doorstep foundling. Eddie and Elizabeth carefully pried nine baby opossums from their dead mother's pouch where they were suckling.

"Since they do suckle inside the pouch until they are sizeable, they were like nine tiny rats. I couldn't tell them apart," said Elizabeth. "So I had to have two incubators (wastebaskets). I sat in the middle of the bed, took one baby out and fed it, put it in the other wastebasket until I had fed all nine, then I started over again. I kept them until they were grown. They weren't getting quite enough vitamins so I took them to the veterinarian. He gave all nine of them shots. We let them loose in different wooded places when they were old enough."

SQUIRRELS

The whole neighborhood knew the Clarksons' succession of squirrels. Monkey the squirrel was playful like a dog or cat especially with ribbons. Another squirrel named Embryo collected treasures. In his special rotten log on the bedroom desk, Elizabeth found, after his death, a thimble, a small pair of scissors, pecans, choice bits he brought home to hide in his private cache.

These squirrels were some of the many brought to the Clarksons' door by the postman or neighbors who found them as tiny, apparently abandoned babies. They knew Elizabeth would know what to do.

The garden itself had a large wild squirrel population. Other than the resounding call of the Carolina wren, the loudest sound in the garden has always been the alarms and sudden shaking of entire, supple trees or limbs as squirrels leap to follow their playful aerial routes. Around Wing Haven's amply supplied feeders, squirrels have long coexisted amicably with birds and chipmunks.

Initially, Eddie tried many schemes to keep the squirrels away before he declared it a near impossibility. Elizabeth prided herself on her invention: "It tells me I am smarter than a squirrel after all. Birds, especially small birds, can use my upstairs window feeder and squirrels cannot get on it."

While raising Sammy, a foundling squirrel, Elizabeth left the upstairs window open with a log in her window near the magnolia tree, so he could come and go as he wished. At night he slept inside the rolled, pink satin comforter at the foot of Elizabeth's bed. That remained his favorite inside place until he built a nest in the bookcase with pink facial tissue. It didn't upset Elizabeth that Sammy chewed several books to hollow them out for nesting in her bookcase. "I believe in a balanced universe. Some books and some animals."

Sammy playfully rolled over, grabbed and chased his tail, and sometimes when a class of children came, he jumped cheerfully on the head or shoulder of each child. He expected kindness and hospitality. Elizabeth was concerned that Sammy in his wider travels might jump on someone in friendship and frighten them, causing the person to retaliate or knock the squirrel down. Then, of course, a squirrel will bite.

Elizabeth acquired the squirrel, Frog Legs, the way she usually got birds and animals. "Often people try to do something with animals on their own and get them in bad condition. When they don't know what to do, they bring it to me. It is much harder then to get them back to health. Orphaned birds and animals are seldom really orphaned. Often the parent will leave a small bird or animal briefly to go in search of food, but will soon return. Meanwhile a well-meaning child will 'rescue' fledglings that are only temporarily abandoned." Elizabeth felt that as long as dogs and cats could be kept away from the small squirrels, patience was usually all that was required.

Elizabeth often raised foundlings brought by personnel from the Charlotte Nature Museum. One tiny squirrel arrived with a bad case of diarrhea. Held in her hand, his small belly turned up and his long legs hanging down, he seemed thin as a small frog, so they called him Frog Legs. Elizabeth worked over him and fed him vitamins until he recovered. One baby squirrel with a broken jaw stayed in Elizabeth's cupped hand for days. She fed him soft foods until his jaw healed and she knew he would survive.

Another baby squirrel brought to the Clarksons stayed in the large, antique rose medallion bowl atop her dining room table. Elizabeth made a soft nest for him there. As soon as he could climb to the top of the nest and look over, she took him out to prevent his falling from the table.

Uncle John, the yard man who worked for the Clarksons until he was 91, rode the city bus home at night and overheard two passengers talking. Listening closer, he realized they were describing the couple in Myers Park who kept a dead tree with branches in an upstairs bedroom to let squirrels run up and down. One rider shook his head. He didn't believe such a tale. "It's true!" Uncle John assured him. "I work for them."

Elizabeth later said, "Because I had bookcases to the ceiling on both sides of my bedroom, I let the squirrels enjoy themselves and exercise. I wouldn't advise anybody to have birds or rabbits or squirrels in the house if they care anything about furniture. I like animals even more than furniture."

COMPANY

or a woman who abhorred both marketing and cooking, Elizabeth Clarkson had an amazing amount of company. Early in her marriage she devised a plan to do her bulk buying four times a year. For small items, Eddie stopped by the market on his way home from work. Elizabeth and Rosetta Roberts and later Elsie Brewer undertook a semi-annual cooking marathon. They cooked seven turkeys, sliced them, and placed slices in juice and gravy into small packages which they labeled as to how many servings were included. Sometimes they froze gravy in ice cube trays, then packaged and stacked "bricks" of gravy in the freezer. Over the years Elsie made thousands of hot, spicy cheese biscuits, which she partially baked and froze by the dozen in freezer bags for instant Clarkson company dinners.

One good friend recalls, "Elizabeth would call us up and say, 'We've just decided to have you over for dinner.' Ten people or so. Elsie served from a huge serving tray that had everything on it. It must have been heavy." Such frequent and consistent hospitality was a studied extension of the welcoming spirit of the garden. Guests felt a sense of harmony, order, well-being, and the quiet vitality of Wing Haven.

Dinner table talk was lively, opinionated, and full of forays into politics, religion, race and divorce, all of which were subjects usually considered mealtime taboo in the 1940s and 50s in the South. Elizabeth read widely and was quite opinionated, as much about politics and social issues as about the colors of her clothing and upholstery. In selecting fabric for chairs, she would buy a yard and live with it across the chair for a month. She spent considerable time choosing fabrics for her own clothes. She always wore pastels and had her shoes dyed to match. She wore the same single piece of jewelry, a large ivory cross from New Orleans. After she got it, she wore it everyday of her life. Once she had something the way she liked it, she never changed it again.

Even for the two of them dining alone in the garden, each meal tray was set with silverware and linen napkins. At both outdoor and indoor dinner parties, the Clarksons used pink damask linen napkins, fingerbowls, and tall, crystal candelabra with hanging cut glass crystals and white candles. As a child seven or eight years old, one Charlottean came often with her family to dinner. She remembers the meals as usually formal. She especially recalls being there when Tommy the bluebird lived in the house. The backs of chairs were covered with cellophane or plastic. "I remember Tommy hiding in the bookcase. He would dart out and land on my chairback or maybe my shoulder. It wasn't the easiest thing to be fairly quiet when I knew Tommy was about. It was wonderful and startling. I never knew what would happen.

"Occasionally there would be a small animal in the Chinese bowl as a centerpiece: once a nest of baby rabbits. I loved to come for supper. At dinner out on the terrace, each chair had a hummingbird feeder attached. As we watched, flocks of birds would gather at the long glass, cylindrical feeders. The terrace came alive with small, darting birds. I'd sit quietly and be part of a magical world. Elizabeth treated children in a special manner. Whatever she had of interest in the garden or house, she let us hold, feel, or smell it.

"Then after dinner, Eddie would take his flashlight, shine it into the grass and pick up little diamond-like eyes shining back at me. They were out there. Elizabeth created an awareness in me that led to a real love for nature and interest in animal life.

"Because of Elizabeth, a neighbor friend and I started a children's bird club which met down by the creek on Thursday afternoons. To learn to identify birds by name, we each spent $5 on bird cards and books. At home we each had bird feeders and watched them all the time.

"People were influenced at Wing Haven. It was the effect she had on us. She made children, workmen, everyone feel so important. Later I recall how she designed the ornate iron gates and explained carefully to the workman what she wanted. He built them precisely like she said."

Besides the presence of Tommy the bluebird during dinner parties or an occasional fledgling in the Chinese bowl, there was usually a resident dog. One, named Shadow, would bring a square of wax paper and lay it on the floor beside the dinner guest's chair. A frequent guest would know to place her dinner scraps on the paper for Shadow.

Elizabeth's niece from Texas visited often as a child. Later she brought her own children. She particularly remembers the hilarity of lighthearted party games as well as the novelty of the Clarksons' household intercom, quite a rare convenience in the 1950s. "I could order what I wanted for breakfast. They'd call up to the bedroom and ask; then we'd join them for breakfast in the garden. They would take turns reading from the Bible and several Episcopal devotional publications. At dinner with Aunt Lib and Uncle Eddie, rabbits and chipmunks came and ate at our feet.

"I remember one of their dogs who took our youngest boy's baby bottle, lay on his back and drank it. We left it for him when we went home. Later when my boys were older and came to visit, Aunt Lib asked them to wear coats and ties to dinner.

But they were also told that Aunt Lib and Uncle Eddie didn't care what they wore beneath the table, so they wore coats, ties, shorts and flip flops.

"And then there was Daphne, a large, white, housetrained rabbit. She chewed on the leg of the Clarksons' Steinway grand piano. It didn't bother Aunt Lib at all."

Small, efficient and purposeful household amenities which impressed the niece were such things as pink packets of sulfa powder, sewed like sachet bags (to rub on ankles to prevent chiggers and insect bites); or in the powder room, scented powder in a salt shaker (to sprinkle for feminine freshening up on hot summer days); an elaborate sewing cabinet hidden entirely in drawer shelves; and an arm hook for opening doors while carrying a tray. Elizabeth's household was as intentional as her garden.

Concert pianist Harriette Line Thompson remembers first meeting Elizabeth when Harriette and her husband were on their honeymoon in 1947. "Sydnor wanted me to meet Elizabeth. She and I had both gone to the New England Conservatory of Music and we had a lot in common. Elsie let us in. I sat in this gorgeous living room looking out back toward the crepe myrtle in bloom, the pink slipcovers done in the same color to match the tree. Elizabeth came downstairs quite like an angel in her filmy aqua dressing gown and aqua slippers.It was about 10 a.m. She later got out the pink mealworm can and birds floated out of the sky into her hand. She invited us back for dinner to see the hummingbirds. There were about forty of them buzzing and divebombing. It was incredible.

"Every time we'd visit I'd give a piano concert at Wing Haven. At the first one, I played Schumann's 'Papillons,' probably a Beethoven sonata, a Chopin etude, and the 'Chromatic Fantasy and Fugue' of Bach. Bach was her favorite.

"We came back to live in Charlotte in 1954, and at her candlelit dinners she wanted me to play. She invited her friends. The garden was her concert hall with the Steinway pulled out

56

onto the terrace. She in her pastels with matching shoes, Eddie wearing white suits all summer, everything was very individual. Nothing she did was like anybody else. When I brought my mother to visit Elizabeth, one of the birds 'performed' on my mother."

For *Charlotte Observer* columnist Dorothy Knox, Wing Haven was a sure bet when she was looking for a column idea. Knox described Tommy the bluebird scolding at length until he got Elsie's attention drawn to a coiled snake that had crawled up the heat vent from the basement. In another column, she described Elizabeth fastening colored cups of sugar water by wires to the terrace bushes, then moving the cups closer. After the hummingbirds got used to them, she moved them even closer to fasten them onto the chairs. "Right beside my shoulder, dozens spinning around me. I could even hear their tiny, incessant chatter."

A parade of noteworthy visitors, including eminent author and naturalist Roger Tory Peterson, came to see the birds at Wing Haven. Some, like *National Geographic* writer and wildlife photographer Fred Truslow, stayed overnight for the full show. Peterson commented, "There is only one other place in America where wild birds are as tame as they are here." Dorothy Doughty arrived in April, 1956 to study the myrtle warblers in the Clarksons' Japanese cherry trees. Doughty, the British ceramic designer for Royal Worcester Porcelain Company, was doing a series of bone china reproductions of American birds. While at Wing Haven, she did an intricate model and study of the myrtle warblers and also studied their Carolina wrens as models for Bewick's wren. Each completed pair of birds took about two years to make. At Tiffany's in 1956, a pair of Doughty's wrens sold for $600. They were produced in limited quantity and each bird handpainted to match Doughty's original. Doughty's Wing Haven myrtle warblers on the Clarksons' living room mantle were the first pair produced. A gift from Doughty, they were the Clarksons' most prized possession.

Other fond reminders in the garden are of guests

not nearly as famous. During World War II, the Clarksons, like many Charlotte families, entertained soldiers in their home. Soldiers at Camp Sutton near Monroe and Morris Field Air Force Base were invited to Wing Haven. Some became lifelong friends. In the war years of the 1940s, Charlotteans frequently invited soldiers home to dinner if they met them uptown, at church, or at a bus stop. Eddie often arrived home with a soldier in tow. Since the Clarksons had no children, they "adopted" several surrogate sons in this manner and corresponded often with them, as well as their wives and mothers for many years.

In appreciation for the Clarksons' hospitality, Reid Smalley sent them a subscription to *Natural History Magazine*. The card announcing the gift had a handsome drawing, "Saint Francis and the Birds." Elizabeth had a sculptress copy the drawing in plaster; then she sent the plaque mold to the Gorham Company in New York to be cast in bronze. It is a focal point of one of the quiet spaces along the garden wall. At another quiet interval stands a statue of St. Fiacre, the patron saint of gardens. At one turn in the path waits a standing St. Therese, the patron saint of roses. At the entrance to the Herb Garden, a marble marker is centered in the brick walkway, its words composed by one soldier guest, Paul Carpenter, who helped Elizabeth in the garden.

Throughout Wing Haven, brief quotations are cast in bronze, carved in marble or in the oak threshold of the door leading to the garden vista. Each invites meditation. From Genesis, Luke, St. Francis, DeLe Quintinye (a seventeenth century French gardener), Toyohiko Kagawa (a Japanese philosopher), poets Christina Rosetti and Elizabeth Barrett Browning, a widely international array of words are integrated into the garden. Elizabeth, from her eclectic reading, would copy a favorite verse, a single phrase or sentence of poetry, scripture, or philosophy. For many years she collected them in a shoebox overflowing with quotations. For birthdays or anniversaries, she or Eddie would order one to be cast and placed strategically in the garden.

The quotations have fascinated generations of schoolchildren, who stop to spell out the words. Adults walking along the paths stop to copy them in checkbooks or on the backs of wallet cards. Biology classes, such as those who came consistently from nearby Queens College, have used the garden plants and wildlife for an extended observatory. Dr. Sara Nooe, professor of Biology at Queens, wrote that some of the young people Elizabeth taught went on to become educators, ornithologists, and wildlife artists.

Many writers came. Some to write articles about the garden itself. Ruth Moose brought her son and wrote, "A woodpecker sat on Mrs. Clarkson's wrist eating from her hand. She said to my son Barry, 'Do you know what a woodpecker's tongue is like?' He didn't. 'It's long and has a rough, spear-like tip on the end. Sometimes when I'm feeding the woodpecker, she will run that tongue around and under my fingernail.'"

Elizabeth Lawrence, who was the Clarksons' long-time Ridgewood Avenue neighbor and visitor, became a widely acclaimed garden writer describing her own garden and Southern gardens. Her lively garden lore and observations reflected a rich familiarity with folklore and literature. Lawrence's classics in American garden writing include *Gardens in Winter, The Little Bulbs, A Southern Garden,* and a popular posthumous book, *Gardening for Love: The Market Bulletins,* edited by *New York Times* garden columnist Allen Lacy.

In 1961, author Lawrence described Wing Haven's familiar terrain: "By night, the water-mirror reflects the stars, by day the clouds, in winter the green branches of pine trees—in spring the pale flower of the weeping cherry. All through the garden there are shallow basins for birds, always with cool, fresh water dripping in and overflowing. In the main garden a formal pool reflects in winter the ivory trunk and branches of a large crepe myrtle, in summer its masses of pink flowers."

Wing Haven
A Sanctuary Continues

harlotte's Sugar Creek and its mosquito-breeding, bottomland marshes lay just below the Clarksons' home and garden. The neighborhood was still country enough to have thickets of blackberry rambling the creekbanks. And it was still peaceful enough to hear the lowing of cows toward milking time from the across-the-creek dairy farm of Frank Graham. (In those days, Graham's son Billy was known only as another neighbor who had done his schoolboy share of the milking.) Many of the Clarksons' neighbors along low-lying Westfield Road, like many Charlotteans, were beseiged with mosquitoes and flies each summer. After the discovery of DDT's effectiveness, they clamored for the DDT trucks to come and spray.

The Health Department fogging truck, which two young workers loaded with DDT and drove each summer weeknight in 1955 through Charlotte neighborhoods, was so popular that people would run out into the street to be sprayed. Some even took off their clothes. The two who drove the noisy truck were given a city map of zoned areas targeted for spraying flies and mosquitoes.

Although the cause of polio had not yet been determined, the crippling polio epidemics of the 1940s were so fresh in public memory that people were eager to avoid potentially disease-bearing insects. The general population celebrated and used DDT widely against lice, flies, and mosquitoes.

When the fogging took place in the late 1940s and again in 1951, 1952 and 1953, Elizabeth Clarkson protested tenaciously and would come out into Ridgewood Avenue in her dressing gown to waylay the approaching truck. "You'll spray my garden over my dead body," she told them. The fogger made a tremendous noise and could be heard blocks away. She feared DDT's lingering influence and what it would do to the creatures in her garden. She saw its immediate and residual effects as few others could.

Elizabeth's complaints to Mayor Herbert Baxter had small effect. The city agreed not to spray her garden and yard, but continued neighborhood spraying. One of the city's sprayers, who was also a medical student and would later become president of the Wing Haven Foundation, recalled, "We had strict rules to cut off the fogger at a certain place near Ridgewood Avenue. We didn't call anybody to tell them we were coming to spray. There was antagonism in the neighborhood. Some insisted that their yards and streets must be sprayed. But we cut off for the Clarksons' property.

"In medical school in 1955 we had a brand new course called Ecology. Nothing was ever mentioned about DDT. Fogging with DDT was well thought of by everyone except Elizabeth Clarkson. She'd be out on the curb in her lovely pink negligee with her hair up in a bun."

The Charlotte Observer reported in June, 1953, that Eddie Clarkson hired lawyer William Poe to argue before City Council against the general DDT fogging of their neighborhood. "After hearing arguments on behalf of 351 petitioners who demanded the fogging in the interest of health, the council referred it to the city manager, directing him to resume. It was understood

62

that the surrounding streets [Selwyn, Westfield, Maryland, and Hillside Avenues] would be sprayed. The fogging was [briefly] stopped in 1948 when Mr. and Mrs. Clarkson complained that birds in their sanctuary were being poisoned by food contaminated by DDT."

In 1958 articles appeared in *Audubon* and *Scientific American* on the residual effects of spraying. But not until Rachel Carson's startling breakthrough book, *Silent Spring*, was published in 1962 did the public begin to learn the widespread effects of DDT. In Carson's chapter "And No Birds Sing," landowners all over America reported total loss of large populations of birds after local spraying. Groundwater and fish showed contamination miles distant from spraying sites. Wide reports were given of birds building nests but laying no eggs, or laying eggs which never hatched.

Elizabeth saw the deadly effects firsthand. One of Wing Haven's catbirds, Mama, always mothered at least three sets of young a year until the DDT spraying began near the garden. After the spraying, the young died before leaving the nest. This happened to Mama repeatedly. And the hummingbirds which had delighted visitors each summer in great numbers almost disappeared. The bluebirds also never resumed their former numbers.

Not until 1972 did the evidence of the concentration of DDT in dangerous accumulations in fish and birds lead the U.S. Government to restrict DDT use. Russell Piethman, director of the Charlotte Nature Museum, described Elizabeth as "among the first to recognize the dangers of DDT to the environment, in her housecoat and slippers, standing guardian of Nature in the middle of Ridgewood Avenue in the early morning hours."

Another dire event called Elizabeth into public notice in 1955. At Charlotte's airport a ceilometer was installed to measure the cloud ceiling above the airport. The extremely large, bright light was aimed straight up at the sky and had a tall metal fence surrounding it.

One night in September during bird migration time,

the clouds formed a low ceiling with a cold front moving in. Police Chief Frank N. Littlejohn called Elizabeth to hurry and help identify birds out at the airport. They were crashing into the ceiliometer fence by the hundreds. Police had thrown bushels of dead birds into the lake. Many were still hanging in the fence. The field was littered with them. The birds had been blinded by the light and had circled and circled, hit the fence and dropped.

The Charlotte Observer contained Elizabeth's sad report: tanangers, orioles, hundreds of warblers died. The most numerous were red-eyed vireos. At the Charleston, Nashville, and Atlanta airports the reports were the same. Thousands of migrating birds were killed. After this incident, the airports began using a black light which does not disorient birds.

Elizabeth brought home some of the dead birds to weigh and identify and to give to the Biology Department at Queens College for study. One red-eyed vireo, which was temporarily blinded, recovered enough to be sent to a warmer climate. A notice appeared in the paper about the vireo's seeking a ride south. No airline would take it, but dozens of travelers called and offered. A truck driver called. He was driving straight through. He carried the red-eyed vireo survivor in a cage and called to say he had released it at Vero Beach, Florida.

Because of the publicity surrounding such events, more and more people learned of Wing Haven and the Clarksons' nurturing concern for birds. Wing Haven became a widely known sanctuary. And the stories about Wing Haven foundlings continued in *The Charlotte Observer*: a trapped baby starling discovered in an uptown postal recruiting office; a set of chimney swift orphans whose nest dislodged and fell in to a family's fireplace.

Because so many people came to see the garden and its wildlife, the Clarksons reluctantly posted public hours on the gate. "Open Monday through Wednesday afternoons 3-5." But often someone knocked who was only in town this one day. The Clarksons rarely refused anyone who wanted to see the garden.

To help with the large flow of people, the Guild of the Charlotte Nature Museum sent volunteers as afternoon hostesses, guides, and docents.

But any morning in the 1960-80s, large groups of adults and students came for scheduled tours. Volunteers with gardening talents assisted in the garden. Some worked during the annual spring House and Garden Tour since Wing Haven was a favorite stop. At the end of student tours, everyone was served kool-aid and a cookie. Almost always, Elizabeth Clarkson talked with the children and fed mealworms to cardinals out of her hand. Dozens of articles appeared in regional newspapers and magazines, written by visiting writers who were captivated by the extraordinary life of the garden and its owners.

One such writer was Bryan Haislip of the *Winston-Salem Sentinel*. He began, "This is a love story. We stopped in Charlotte to see a friend. She said, 'Come with me to Wing Haven. I have to do some watering.' We met the Clarksons who were dressed in white as is their custom this season. Singly and together, they have an elegance and civility which seems of another age. They are sophisticated in the true sense: their manners are not artificial, but inherent in giving others respect and the expectation of friendship. They treat the natural world in just the same way. They are as polite to a bird as they would be to a person."

At a dinner party in the late 1960s, the Clarksons sat talking with their hosts, who were longtime friends and supporters of Wing Haven. Their host asked a question, "What do you plan to do with your garden?" Subsequently a young attorney and his wife, close friends of the Clarksons, talked with them over many dinner gatherings about the future of Wing Haven and the need for its preservation. During these conversations, Eddie stated he had discussed leaving Wing Haven to a national nature organization, but was told that this organization would probably sell Wing Haven to fund other projects. The young lawyer told Eddie, that contrary to other advice, there was a way for Wing Haven to become an eleemosynary institution. As a friend of the Clarksons, he contributed his legal skills to form Wing Haven Foundation. The Foundation would keep the garden open for the public and operate it in the same manner and purpose as the Clarksons. In 1975 the remainder of the garden, excluding the house, was deeded to the Foundation.

As the manpower and financial requirements of tending a three-acre garden escalated, the Foundation members in the early 1980s sought a broader base of support. A thirteen minute film narrated by national television personality Dick Cavett was produced and shown widely for fundraising and awareness purposes. "Wing Haven: A Gift To A City" showed foresight on the part of the Foundation Board, because operating expenses for the garden continued to grow. In 1983 the Foundation hired a director to help the Clarksons manage the garden and to learn from them how they wanted Wing Haven to be perpetuated.

In 1987 the Foundation raised $430,000 in pledges during a capital fund campaign. That year a garden shop, established in the late 1970s by the Wing Haven Society, raised over $20,000 from sales to help sustain the garden. The Clarksons also completed their gift in 1987 by giving two houses which are situated among the gardens. By this time the total gift was complete—two homes and almost four acres.

At home, in October, 1988, Elizabeth Clarkson died. A strange emptiness lay along the street and within the house and garden. Fortunately, the stable plan for funding, the small staff, volunteers, and public support were well in place. Her death did not mean the closing of Wing Haven. She and Eddie had been able to remain in their generous, much-beloved home with its garden-filled windows and hundreds of birds on their windowsills. Eddie subsequently moved to a retirement home. And Wing Haven continued.

But no one could foresee the sudden catastrophe of September, 1989, when Hurricane Hugo struck Charleston, South

Carolina and hurled its full-powered maverick path inland to Charlotte. The next morning Wing Haven garden looked devastated. Many great shade trees lay uprooted, bent and twisted, strewn like match sticks across pools and dormant beds of wildflowers. The carefully, frugally built wall, which had grown in slow, painful stages, stood gaping in many places under fallen trees. Miraculously only one tall cedar rested gently on the roof edge of the house, just missing the chimney.

One friend of the garden observed that after the hurricane, she could clearly see "the wonderful bones of the garden." Elizabeth's farsighted garden plan, classic and original, lay exposed in a manner she never imagined. The sudden absence of tree cover made the feat of the Clarksons' effort even more impressive. Her design was a cross of Lorraine laid on its side (++) with the house settled into the lower middle space formed by the cross. The upper garden to the east, where the Clarksons always began their walks, ended at the large pool in the lower garden west of the house. Cross paths offered surprising glimpses and color.

By spring of 1990, after over $50,000 in tree removal and repairs, the garden opened again on the first of May. The verses inscribed throughout the garden were undamaged. The cycle of rebirth began once more, almost as though nothing had happened. The birds returned as always. Only the wood ducks were initially hesitant. For the first time in many years the roses had enough sun. Even the shady glade of Frog Hollow lay partially open to light. An article, which ironically appeared in that May's *Victoria* magazine, featured photos of Wing Haven's previous summer's vast depths of shade. In time these will return. By the summer following the hurricane, the meandering rear path once again wandered through natural woods where goldenseal, jonquils, scilla, trillium and snowdrops burst through a blanket of wild ginger. Once again in summer the old-fashioned colors of plumbago, crinum lily and cleome spilled softly onto the garden grass.

Wing Haven, like its extraordinary creator,

Elizabeth Clarkson, is resurgent and remarkable. A gentle lady possessed of fierce determination, Elizabeth Clarkson very purposefully set out in the 1920s to live a most unusual life. In the process she created a garden and focused her life there, using her exceptional talent for design and for the nurture of plants and animals. With singular vision, she and Eddie Clarkson transformed "a hopeless plot of clay" into a magnificent garden. Because of the beauty of the garden and the grace with which they lived, their friendships extend worldwide and draw visitors continually to Wing Haven.

"Although the busy world of a big city whirls around you, Wing Haven's quietness seeps into you the moment you step inside the brick walls. You lower your voice, slow your steps, and leave your anxieties outside the tall iron gate." *

CONVERSATION

itting on the living room sofa, Elizabeth wore a simple aqua dress, her white hair upswept with combs, her eyes lively and mischievous, and her manner gracious after even the fiftieth guest. For a a few moments the doorbell was silent and we were the only two people in the house and garden.*

Fresh, pink roses in a crystal vase just inside the front door graced a glass-topped table with pale seashells, letters, and a tiny pink can of mealworms for the cardinals. On every surface were books and momentoes. Through the wide doorway on the long, cushioned window seat lay several pair of binoculars for visitors to closely watch birds on the pool and at the many feeders. "The wood ducks came earlier," she said as she pointed to pine siskins and purple finches.

Question: Do you really treat animals as persons?

Elizabeth: Yes. They are my guests. I try to make my animals and birds comfortable, if I know what they want. I've done it so long I usually know what they need. You get an inner feeling and you can tell if a bird doesn't feel well, if a bird wants something that it doesn't have, some kind of freedom it wants. If anybody adjusts, it's me. (She laughs.) Honestly, if I had to do without food to feed a bird or animal that I loved, I would.

Q. Aren't these extraordinary means to go to for animals—things other people don't or won't do?

E. No, they don't have time and they won't take the time. I really didn't have time either, but I took the time because it seemed important to me.

Q. And you know what to do.

E. No, you just have to trust in the Lord and do the best you can. Of course, I have always tended to animals. Eddie says the first date he had with me in Boston, I told him about Mother and my raising white winged doves and how they would take things from my lips, and fly against the screen to come in. Eddie knew what he was up against. We had squirrels and other small animals in our house in Texas.

Q. Even if Eddie suspected what he was in for, do you think he expected grubworms being beaten up on the bed, as the bluebird Tommy did to soften them?

E. (Laughing) He can take almost anything. He's adaptable.

Q. What was your Mother like?

E. She was always interested in everything that was going on. Once she saw a lot of specks in the cat's bed and said, "You know, I want to find out what those things are." So she put them in a Mason jar and they hatched into fleas. She had the same kind of curiosity I have. When we dug our well here, I put the dirt from the drill hole in glass jars. I wanted to see what was under me.

Q. Did your Mother have a reverence for life like you have?

E. Yes. Once she even gave a chicken an enema.

Q. Did you grow up on a farm?

E. We lived right in the heart of town in Uvalde, Texas, right on the corner on a long, deep lot. We faced the Baptist church across the street. To the side was a Methodist church, and right behind, the Christian Science church, and right behind us the Mexican Catholic church, a block down was the Presbyterian and cattycornered a block away the Episcopal church with its steeple. We went to church in self defense, because if they all got to singing at one time,

72

it was something else.

Q. You had a garden?

E. When I was married, Mother had the whole yard planted in poppies and larkspur and lots of roses. Before I was born, she had over a thousand roses, but when I was a little girl, she had a great many which grew very large trunks. In those days they didn't prune severely. Mother let her poppies and larkspur go to seed, then she gathered the dry seed and threw them along Texas roadsides. For many years you could see them growing.

Q. What did you play as a child?

E. We had tiny white pebbles and I laid out houses and rooms with them, then gardens with all its patches in pebbles. I really think that's more where I got my talent for architecture, because that was more fun than dolls. I never played dolls. I made clothes for them, then put them on the shelf naked. My Mother thought there was something terribly wrong with me. I had these expensive dolls I loved, made clothes for them, then folded the clothes, put the dolls up undressed, and went to play baseball. I was embarrassed because Mother called me in. She was so afraid I would break a finger and not be able to play the piano. Mother found out that when she asked me to do something I didn't want to do, I'd start practicing. But when I got older, nobody had to tell me to practice.

Q. Did you want to be a pianist?

E. I didn't want to be a concert pianist. I just wanted to be as good a pianist as I could be and I think I probably was at one time.

Q. When you designed this house in 1926, you obviously designed it to bring the outdoors in. Was this an idea from very far back?

E. Absolutely. Our house in Texas was full of windows. The library had four regular windows. Our front door was bevelled glass. I expect psychologically I got a lot of ideas from my own past.

Q. Was the idea of visually bringing the outside in pretty rare then?

E. Mother would not have curtains over the windows like everybody else. When I was a child, I thought it was just awful that we didn't have curtains.

Q. All those church people looking in?

E. She said if you want privacy, pull down the shade, but she wanted to see out. When Eddie and I moved into this house, I wouldn't even hang pictures. I wanted to make a picture out of every window.

Q. Did you have a garden when you were young?

E. I never gardened at home. I didn't know anything about it. Mother was the gardener and had a Mexican gardener to help. So I never planted things except just before I was married, I got interested. Then I ordered gladiola bulbs. I couldn't have done anything better, because you don't do a thing to them, just put them in the ground where it is warm and sunny, they will come up and bloom beautifully. If you want to start a child off, choose the right kind for pure sun and warm temperature at the right time, because children can see the tops come up immediately. Much prettier than watching lettuce grow.

Q. Did you have animals when you were young?

E. I had a raccoon and my brothers had a coyote before my time. They were much older, so I didn't know the coyote or the bull. One of the cutest pets I ever had was a squirrel named Curley. We let him go in and out of the house always. He slept in the boys' pockets and Dad's suit pockets hanging in the closet. At the time I was married, I had two squirrels and Mother had a big cage built, a room-sized cage. It was eight-sided, covered with wire and the top came to a point. Years later Mother just got tired of fooling with them. I happened to be reading the town paper and saw that Mrs. Barnhill had given the two seventeen-year-old squirrels to the park. I was quite upset. The squirrels did just what I thought they would do. The Mexicans had to shoot them because they didn't know how to care for themselves. They were red fox squirrels.

Years after we had those squirrels, Mother found pecans they had hidden down in the bedsprings, those open bedsprings that curled down to a little point. Mother was as crazy about animals as I am. The collie she bred was so much a part of the family, that she had a coffin built for him and he was buried on the cemetery lot with the rest of the Barnhills.

Q. Can you explain the extraordinary presence people feel in your garden?

E. Once I felt led to do the garden in a certain way, I never moved it. It is exactly what was planned to begin with. The garden's not finished. If I had a lot of money, I'd have done a great deal more. But we always did everything on a shoestring. Eddie never made a lot of money, so we were never wealthy, but we lived wealthy.

74

Q. Like using fingerbowls at meals, for instance?

E. Always for lunch and dinner, yes.

Q. As you get older, do material things become less important?

E. Not to me. I have great sentiment about everything I have. I love all these chairs. They are fine except these. This was a rocker. I sawed the legs off a radio. Remember when radios had legs? I put them on the rocker, covered it to the ground and no one ever knew whose legs it had. I have lots of fun making do.

Q. Do you plan your days as you did your house?

E. I used to make menus two weeks ahead. We had to have something different every morning. Now we eat the same thing day after day.

Eddie comes home to lunch daily. That was one of the things I required of my husband. I said, "You have to come home for lunch every day and take a nap." At first he carried on. I said, "Lie down for fifteen minutes; you don't have to do anything else." Finally he got used to it and liked it.

The reason I did that was my father, one of the healthiest people I ever saw. He'd come home, say, "Lilly, is lunch ready?" If it wasn't, he'd never stop. He'd pick up the hoe he kept at the back door and go out and work his vegetable garden for five or ten minutes, come back, wash his hands, and by that time, lunch would be ready. After lunch, he'd lie down and sleep fifteen minutes and be refreshed. He was a very active man and I never heard him say he was tired.

Q: Could you grow all kinds of vegetables in Uvalde?

E: Oh yes. My grandfather John Claybourne Crisp was a doctor and lived in Uvalde. He came to Texas in the mid-1880s, had been born in Mississippi and his ancestors were early Scotch-Irish settlers in North Carolina. He was the first person to my knowledge in that part of the country to have a vegetable garden. It was very dry during that period and his youngest boy would carry water to the garden. Everyone coming from church walked by to see the vegetable garden. They'd never seen one. I don't know what they ate.

Q: Before you were married, did you have a plan for your life as well as your house?

E. I did plan the way I wanted to live, how I wanted things served and how I wanted to shop. I knew I didn't want to shop every day. I used to shop just four times a year, but I know mothers with teenagers can't do that. And we had quite a vegetable garden. Eddie loves to shop and he does it now.

Q: Shopping takes your time away from more important things?

E. Yes, from things I want to do like the garden.

Q: You are so ladylike and always wear a dress and stockings. What did you used to look like when you were working on pools, laying brick walks and digging?

E. I never had garden clothes. Once when I said, "I've got to make some housedresses," a friend asked, "What do you consider a housedress?" Well, I told her, something attractive and comfortable in a hammock. We always have one. I have never changed clothes to garden. I wear the same things I put on to go out. They're not fine things. I don't get myself terribly dirty. A gardener friend says "You just don't work! I've never caught you working!" She wears blue jeans and wipes her hands on them, and thinks everybody has to wear something like that in order to garden, but I never did.

I used to put a mild soap all over my hands and it was easier to get the dirt off. I'm not as active a gardener, of course, as I was. I wouldn't think anything of filling a wheelbarrow full of dirt, but I'm not that foolish now. [1978]

Q: How old are you?

E. 73

Q: What are your goals or projects for the future?

E: I would like to do a lot for the garden, and not change anything about the house except to renew things.

Q: How did you and Eddie and later your friends come to give garden related gifts instead of a dress, perfume, a trip or ordinary presents?

E: I remember when we were first married, we gave each other the usual things. Before I was married, a friend's husband gave her a beautiful chair. I thought that was a shame, giving something so practical. Later when I wanted all these things for the garden and we wouldn't get them any other way, we gave each other bricks and boxwood or azaleas or whatever we wanted. I once got 10,000 mealworms for a present.

Friends would also give practical things. During World War II the nicest thing they would give me was sugar, because if you had many children, your ration allowed you too much. But with just the two of us, we never did have enough for the hummingbirds. We saved our whole ration for them. One year it took over 200 pounds of sugar because we had so many coming here. We tried honey and other things, but the hummingbirds were spoiled on sugar. We had sixty to seventy-five during April-September in the garden at that time. Enormous crowds of people would come to see them before migration. But after they sprayed DDT in the fifties, we never had so many again.

Q: Your eyes keep going to the windows and beyond to the garden. Do you spend your day oriented outward?

E: I probably do. Even when I am in bed, I have a big mirror at the foot of my bed and across from that, a mirror. I can see the whole garden, the crepe myrtle in bloom, the vitex tree, the magnolia and two windows on the side together where I have the long feeder. I love to read in bed.

Q: Having created a place like this consciously, you must be aware of the different feeling people get coming here to your home and garden, a different sense from other streets nearby?

E: I'm not sure that I do. People come in and say, "This is just another world." I may not realize it because I am in that world all the time and it doesn't seem too different. Of course, most people don't live out in the yard. That is different.

Q: This place is so much like yourself, do you ever think of losing it, of having to leave it?

E: Everybody thinks about that. I just hope that they won't put me somewhere I can't have birds or a dove. I would fight like a wolf.

A friend asked me as we stood in the garden one lovely spring day, "You don't want to go to heaven, do you?" I told him not while my cherry trees are in blossom.

Q: Would you think of heaven in terms of a garden?

E: I don't believe in the regular kind of heaven and hell that most people believe in, not as a place. But I thoroughly believe in an afterlife. If I ever had any doubts about it, they went away when my father was visiting in 1953.

Everything was just right that Christmas Eve. We had sixty people for dinner and my Father sang carols as loudly as anybody. He was a small man and I remember his going up the stairs to his room that night with all his packages the guests had brought.

The next morning I got up early to attend the eight o'clock service. I fixed his oatmeal. He sat right here and the Carolina wren came down and lit on the candles and on the Christmas tree. He enjoyed her so much. We were to go out for a family dinner at 2. He never kept anybody waiting, but he said he was tired and stood here in his overcoat ready to go. He was very meticulous, but I noticed he had buttoned his overcoat wrong. I knew that never happened before on any day of his life.It happens to Eddie all the time, but you know people are different. I said, "Dad, you don't feel very well, do you?" And he said, "No, not very well." I had never heard him say that either, so I said, "Well, we won't go. I'm tired too."

He lay down and I could see it wasn't quite right. I couldn't get a doctor to come. Nobody wants to come out at lunchtime Christmas Day. But he died.

It was just like, do you remember Enoch in the Bible? I was holding his hand and like Enoch, he "walked with God and was not." I am sure there is an afterlife because I saw it then.

Q: He moved somewhere else?

E: Yes, he did.

Eddie came home for lunch. He was courtly, romantic, a smiling, soft-spoken gentleman who in summer wears a fresh rose in the lapel of his white suit. At age 78 he sat in a white wrought-iron chair in the garden and spoke of his life with Elizabeth and what it was like to maintain a very private-public garden.

Q: Is this what you wanted? Do you ever question the garden's taking over your life?

Eddie: I wouldn't trade it for anything I know of. I like the people and excitement of living here and walking out and having a bird light on my hand.

Q: Looking back, this dream you had together, has it taken shape as you imagined?

Eddie: Oh yes and more so. I never thought it would be as beautiful as it is. She says, "You shouldn't brag on it." I say I can because I didn't build it. She designed and built it.

One day just as I was leaving home after lunch, the phone rang. A man asked if I would wait for him. He was coming right over. Someone had just described this place to him and he had to see why it sounded so familiar. He came and told me, "Ever since I was a child, I've been hunting this place. Would you walk around with me?" After we did, he said, "This is the place. I may not be back for awhile, but this eases my mind to have found it."

Elizabeth: We've had others who say they came here with their cub scout troop or kindergarten and have been looking for it ever since. They have no idea where it is or what it's called.

Q: Don't all these people dropping by to see the garden intrude on your privacy?

Elizabeth: It does on Sundays and Saturdays in particular. The sign which tells which afternoons the garden is open doesn't make a bit of difference to many people. And you hesitate to turn them down because you're afraid that's just the person who needs the garden most.

A lady came through and said, "Is this your garden?" I said yes. She burst out crying, "It's just what I've wanted all my life." She didn't look like she'd had very much. I walked out to the car with her. She came back again for several years. You never know who most needs the serenity of a garden.

Q: Do such things happen often? What is a typical day at Wing Haven?

Elizabeth: No day is typical except that the telephone rings all the time.

Q: Calling about problems with birds?

Elizabeth: Yes, all the time. Callers want to know how to care for hurt birds, or what is the name of the bird they just saw. They had the most outrageous descriptions you can imagine. There never was a bird on land or sea like that, but usually, if they have observed carefully, I can figure it out by asking questions.

When children first gather around the sundial by the front door courtyard, they look up at the medium size house which is almost covered with luxurious layers of flowers, shrubs, and trees. They look at the bevelled glass of the arched front doorway and the antique English sundial dated 1705. When Elizabeth came out to greet them, as she usually did, they often asked, "Are you rich?"

She always answered yes. "If you are enjoying yourself and friends, family, and a garden, you are rich. You definitely are."

ACKNOWLEDGEMENTS

The author expresses special thanks to The Wing Haven Foundation, to Sally and Henry James, Ann and John Glover, Wanny Hogewood, Peggy Culbertson, Bill and Elizabeth Ross, Miriam Herin, Dal Shefte, and many others whose generous interviews, writings, assistance, and support made this book possible.

*FOOTNOTES

p. 68 Moose, Ruth, "The World at Wing Haven." *Wildlife in North Carolina* (1972):10,11.

p. 71 Chapter 6. Interviews conducted in 1978 by Mary Kratt.

SELECTED SOURCES

Broley, Myrtle. "Wing Haven." *Nature* 49(Aug-Sept.1956):357-60.

Clarkson, Elizabeth Barnhill. *Birds of Charlotte and Mecklenburg County, North Carolina*. Charlotte: Dowd Press. 1944. "Wing Haven." *Audubon* 47 (July-Aug.1945):230-33.

Vaughan, Ira. "A Gentle Refuge: Wing Haven Gardens." *Victoria* (June 1990):66-75.

Whiteside, Katherine. "Wing Haven." *House and Garden* (June, 1987):167-73, 214-15.

Wright, Leslie. "Wing Haven: Serene Eden in Bustling Charlotte." *Southern Accents* (May-June,1987):152-7.

Newspapers:

Borden, Pat. "Bricks Take Wing To Build Birds' Haven." *Charlotte Observer* (April 15, 1973):1E,2E.

Gary, Kays. "Wing Haven: A Celebration of Life." *Charlotte Observer* (October 10,1988):5D.

Mellnik, Ted. "Wing Haven Celebrates 60th Year." *Charlotte Observer* (April 27, 1987):1B.

Olson, Karen. "Elegant Match Flourishes 50 years." *Charlotte Observer* (April 24, 1977):1E,11E.

Perlmutt, David. "Elizabeth Clarkson Dies." *Charlotte Observer* (October 10, 1988):1D, 5D.

Editorial. *Charlotte Observer* (October 11, 1988):18A.